THE STUDENT'S MUSIC LIBRARY
Edited by Percy M. Young, M.A., D.Mus.

METHOD IN ORCHESTRATION

METHOD IN ORCHESTRATION

by

IAN PARROTT, M.A., D.Mus.

Professor of Music in the University College of Wales, Aberystwyth

FOREWORD BY EDMUND RUBBRA

London
DENNIS DOBSON

First published in Great Britain in 1957 by DOBSON
BOOKS LTD, London, W.8. *All rights reserved*.
Printed in Great Britain by BRISTOL TYPESETTING
COMPANY, Stokes Croft, Bristol 1.

CONTENTS

FOREWORD

IT HAS BEEN my experience that, in books dealing
with the craft of music, the awkward question is hardly
ever taken into account. No such criticism can be made
against the present book. Professor Parrott has been at
pains to push back the frontiers of its subject-matter, so
that a wide range of related topics is brought into view.
Orchestration is then seen as an exciting adventure that
leads us far beyond mere instrumentation.

I have read this book with great interest and enjoyment.

EDMUND RUBBRA.

I

INTRODUCTION

LET US IMAGINE that you are taking on your first job, it may be as a school teacher with music as one of your subjects, or it may be a job quite unconnected with music but one which gives you scope, as an enthusiastic amateur, to organize some practical music-making.

The headmaster, or the local welfare officer, or the vicar, informs you that there are a number of people anxious to form themselves into an orchestra. What can you do about it? You discover that there are half-a-dozen violinists and a problematical double bass player who, having broken one of his strings, has tied it up in a knot and broken it again. The local postmaster plays the bassoon but cannot achieve less than a 'mezzoforte' or more than an 'andante commodo'. You've heard also that you might get a trumpeter who likes dance-music best and a clarinet player who has an obsolete instrument. The village hall—which is next to a fairground—contains a harmonium which is slightly sharp and a piano which is slightly flat.[1]

Can you cope with this?

There are a number of things which you have got to know before you reach the stage of standing up in front of any orchestra; and then, as Sir Hugh Allen once said,

---

[1] See *The Physics of Music* by A. Wood (Methuen, 1944) and the *Music Book* Vol. VII, p. 233, 'A History of Musical Pitch' by W. L. Sumner (Hinrichsen, 1952) for details of rise and fall with temperature change.

'Any fool can get up and wag a stick at an orchestra—and too many fools do.' Sir Adrian Boult, speaking to students of the Birmingham School of Music in 1949, pointed out that conducting, unlike most other aspects of the musical profession, was learnt 'on the job'. It was only by being let loose on an orchestra that the conductor was able to acquire the necessary experience—and he could go on learning all his life. There is, nevertheless, a great deal which can and must be learnt before the budding conductor meets the long-suffering orchestra and though a book can never be a substitute for practical experience it can be a guide.

Of course the musical director must know more about the subject than any of the people he directs. This is not analogous to the situation of the young medical student who having passed his exam said, 'Now for forgetting half I ever learnt.' It is not just a matter of 'standing' or prestige. The immediate usefulness of a theoretical subject may not always be apparent but it should be *useful*. By studying sixteenth century counterpoint, for example, the musician is getting to know a period of history, its resources and aims, which may be quite different from his favourite (which may be that of Chopin). Thus his approach to different music is more broad, tolerant and understanding.

The facility acquired in working exercises in counterpoint moreover will give him not only a sense of discipline and logic but a greater sympathy and understanding towards the contrapuntal devices of other times. It will become noticeably pertinent when he is arranging piano music for instruments; that which may be tolerated by a pianist's left hand may be quite intolerable to an individual cellist in an orchestra, quite apart from its technical suitability to the new instrument. A knowledge

10

of harmony also will be quite indispensable before orchestration and conducting are tackled, and it is for this reason that a fair amount of space, particularly in Chapter III, will be devoted to this matter.

Overleaf are the names of the instruments of the orchestra, in the order of a full score down the page, and some directions for playing, in four languages. These are not all *exact* translations; they are more the *equivalent* words used in each country. Gaps indicate that though a word may be available, a foreign word is generally used.

The scoring is indicated by figures for each group, wood-wind and brass first: e.g. 2121 2230 Perc.Harp.Str.: This means two flutes, one oboe, two clarinets, one bassoon, two horns, two trumpets, three trombones[1] (*no* tuba) percussion, harp and strings, which is—or, perhaps, should be—regarded as a normal *Theatre Orchestra*. 2222 4331 Perc.Harp.Str. is a modest *Symphony Orchestra*. In addition it is usual for the second flute to play piccolo when needed—this is called 'doubling'—the second oboe plays, or doubles, cor anglais, the second clarinet doubles bass clarinet and the second bassoon doubles double bassoon. The second player usually does this duty, as the first player at the desk is a specialist (or soloist) and does not want to spoil his fingering or blowing by changing instruments, when there are solos to be tackled. When there is triple wood-wind, the third player does the doubling.

Now we must get down to examining music in relation to this complicated machine.

---

[1] If three trombones are not available, the scoring will probably be for *one* rather than two.

11

THE INSTRUMENTS OF THE ORCHESTRA

Recommended Abbrev.	Italian		German		French	English
Fl.	Flauto	-i	Flöte	-n	Flûte	Flute
Picc.	Flauto piccolo[1]	-i.-i	Kleine Flöte		Petite flûte	Piccolo
Ob.	Oboe		(H)oboe	-n	Hautbois	Oboe
C.A.	Corno Inglese	-i.-i	Englisches Horn (or Alt-hoboe)	Hörner	Cor Anglais	Cor Anglais (or English Horn)
Cl.	Clarinetto	-i	Klarinette	-n	Clarinette	Clarinet
Cl.B.	Clarinetto basso (or Clarone)		Bassklarinette	-n	Clarinette basse	Bass Clarinet
Fag.	Fagotto	-i	Fagott	-e	Basson	Bassoon
Cfg.	Contrafagotto		Kontrafagott		Contrebasson	Double Bassoon
Cor.	Corno	-i	Horn	Hörner	Cor	(French) Horn
	Corno ventile		Ventilhorn	-hörner	Cor chromatique (à pistons)	Horn (with valves)
Tba.	Tromba	-e	Trompete	-n	Trompette	Trumpet
Tbne.	Trombone	-i	Posaune	-n	Trombone	Trombone
	Tuba	-e	Basstuba	-tuben	Tuba	Tuba
Timp.	Timpani		Pauken		Timbales	Kettledrums
G.C.	Gran Cassa		Grosse Trommel	-n	Grosse Caisse	Bass Drum
	Piatti		Becken		Cymbales	Cymbals
Tamb. picc.	Tamburo piccolo	-i	Kleine Trommel	-n	Tambour militaire	Side Drum
	Tamburino		Schellentrommel		Tambour de Basque	Tambourine
	Campanelle, Campane		Glocken		(Cloches)	Tubular Bells
	Campanetta		Glockenspiel		(Carillon)	Glockenspiel, Chimes
	Arpa		Harfe	-n	Harpe	Harp
Vi.	Violino	-i	Violine	-n	Violon	Violin
Va.	Viola	-e	Bratsche	-n	Alto	Viola
Vcl.	Violoncello	-i	Violoncell	-e	Violoncelle	Violoncello
Cb.	Contrabasso	-i	Kontrabass	-bässe	Contrebasse	Double Bass

[1] The Italians prefer the word 'ottavino'.

ORCHESTRAL DIRECTIONS [1]

Arco	Bogen		Bowed
Pizzicato			Plucked
Sul ponticello		Sur le chevalet	Bowed near the bridge
Con sord(ino)	Dämpfer auf (strings)	Metez les sourdines	Put on mutes
	gestopft (wind)	avec les sourdines	Muted
Senza sord	Dämpfer weg (fort)	ôtez les sourdines	Take off mutes
	ohne Dämpfer	sans	Unmuted
Divisi	Geteilt	Divisés	Playing more than one part
Tutti	Zusammen	Unis	All (or both) playing the same part
Unisoni(a 2)		à deux	
Sul G.	G Saite	corde de Sol	On the G string
Sul IV			On the fourth string

[1] See also Appendix I, *The Grammar of Music* by Hilda Hunter, in this series.

13

II

STATICS AND DYNAMICS

1.   Whether our student is going to arrange something for his own small orchestra or whether he is going to time something for recording or broadcasting, it is clear that he can easily make a bloomer by failing to realize (a) 'static' effects, i.e. the change of colour of a written sound transferred from one medium to another and (b) progression effects, i.e. the movement from one chord to the next (for which a knowledge of harmony is necessary).

Regarding (a) above, consider for a moment the following:

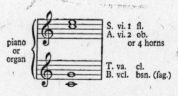

EXAMPLE 1

2.   How inadequate and 'static' this is! How long and how loud should the notes be sounded? Then who shall perform it? Supposing we adopt a moderate degree of
14

loudness and a matter of three or four seconds for the duration, first let us suppose it to be played on the piano. An *advantage* of the piano is that, given an adequate player, the notes can all have the same intensity and the same quality; a *disadvantage* is that they all start dying away as soon as they are struck (which happens in the case of no other important modern instrument except the harp). If it is played on the organ, the notes will have an inhuman precision and will remain inflexibly the same so long as the keys remain depressed. Now suppose it to be sung by voices. Here our uniformity of tone disappears. The tenors and basses will have a robustness in their higher register which, while being fairly matched by the contraltos, will not be quite so well balanced by the sopranos. A slight sound of strain on the tenor G will be apparent also in most amateur choirs unless they sing falsetto. Transfer this chord to a string quartet and all that vocal intensity vanishes. A certain casual sweetness takes its place. The cello is playing on its top string, the viola on its D string and the two violins both on their A strings, unless an open E is called for. It will be noticed that while all players put in a conscientious vibrato, the three upper instruments submerge their personalities into the chord, while the cello remains rather aloof. If you give the chord to flute, oboe, clarinet and bassoon, the first note you will notice is the higher C, since the tone of the oboe is the most penetrating. The note which will be *least* prominent will be the G in the most ineffective register of the clarinet.

Give the chord to four horns and now it will be the top note which will stand out. The first horn will give much the same strained impression on the E (which will have to be written as B, a fifth higher, if he is playing the usual horn in F) as the tenors did on their G. In fact

15

one more note in either case and you have the tenor's
famous (but exceptional) top A and the horn's top C
(which sounds like F to everyone else)! Students are
sometimes impatient to learn the compass of an instrument thinking that it will be sufficient for their needs. Not
only have I tried to show that one simple 'static' chord
changes completely according to its instrumentation, but
it has been shown also that the compass of instruments is
a subtle matter requiring much study. For the moment
then the top note of the tenor voice is G and the top note
of the horn is E (written as B above the treble staff) and
the student should test the advisability of writing higher,
preferably by using his own voice (basses and contraltos
can use D as their starting point instead of G).

A striking way of appreciating some of the above
points in real music is to compare oboes and horns on
precisely the same chord in 'Venus' from Holst's *The
Planets* (at the first andante). By the sheer difference of
tone quality, you would hardly realise that 'theoretically'
the chord is the 'same' in both cases (E.H.=cor anglais[1]):

EXAMPLE 2
Holst, *The Planets, II, Venus* 1914-16

[1] The notes are written a fifth higher than they sound.

16

3. It will be advisable to consolidate here some of the points already made.

It should be remembered that a note written, with or without a metronome indication, for pianoforte or lute, guitar, harp, harpsichord, clavichord or percussion instruments, gives a clear indication of when it should start but not always any more. If the note is a short one, the raising of the finger from the pianoforte keyboard at the end of the note sends the damper back on to the string, stopping the sound. With a longer note this damping effect may be hardly noticeable, because of the important 'dying away' effect (common to all the instruments mentioned above). If passages of so-called 'pianoforte cantabile' are transferred to other instruments a complete change of character must be expected. The effect of the pianoforte pedal must also be considered but as this involves a study of harmony, its discussion will be reserved to the next chapter.

The transitory effect of the piano is both a beauty and a delusion. The Tchaikovsky song, 'A Broken Tryst', ends on a second inversion and one cannot be sure whether this is not a deliberate vagueness where the root, recently played, is still heard in the head or even half-pedalled into the last chord. There is little room for such vagueness in the orchestra. Listen carefully, for example, to the last chord of the slow movement of Beethoven's Eighth Symphony. This is clearly a second inversion even though one retains a memory of the bass note. The last chord of Fauré's *Requiem*, 1888 (a beautiful, but peculiarly scored work), presents a problem. The written effect is that the vocal bass sounds lower than the lowest sustained note on the organ, making a second inversion, like the Beethoven—this is unless the organist draws out a 16ft. stop, which would unduly thicken the texture. In

17

performance, however, it is singularly difficult to hear an inversion, because voices, even deep bass ones, have a tendency to sound *above* instruments.

4. On other instruments, not only are the sounds sustained but even a crescendo can be made on a single note. An important distinction between wind instruments and all others is that the wind players must have rests in which to breathe. The strings are able to keep fresh for longer periods—they do not get puffed—and, as the bulk of the music can be written for them, they are often thought of as the backbone of the orchestra. They can certainly perform some of the most difficult music.

Let us look a little further at the contrast between wind and strings by taking the following quotation.

EXAMPLE 3

Elgar, *The Dream of Gerontius,* opening bars, 1900

5. Here is a typical example of 'blended' scoring. Instead of the primary colours of Handel's time the composer is using secondary colours by mixing his instruments. The student, it is expected, will be practising score-reading as he goes along. The Holst passage, Example 2, should have been readily assimilated and it should be possible to play the chord on the piano, noting the transpositions.

Now a mere glance at Example 3 should be sufficient for the practising score-reader to observe that it is all one tune 'in theory'; that is, you could play it all with one hand (without actually moving the position of the hand) at the piano. But how completely the piano fails to give you the 'colour' of the passage! Four wood-wind players and about eight viola players are playing 'in unison'.

6.   If we imagine first that it is clarinets only, there is a small point to consider: two clarinets, the normal number in an orchestra, are both to play. That is what the 'a 2' means. They sound quite different from *one* clarinet. Listen to the opening of Tchaikovsky's Fifth Symphony for this effect and note also the richness of the tone-colour. Here also are clarinets playing well down in their chalumeau register (the lower twelfth of the compass) and producing a characteristically full-blooded sound. The question which might be asked here is, 'Why are they Clarinets in A?' It is assumed that the student appreciates the basic fact that clarinets are made in two normal sizes, in B flat and in A, and that the choice would normally be made according to the key of the passage. Now transposing instruments are named with reference to the note C, so that in fact when they play this note they sound their 'name-note' instead. That is what being 'in' B flat or A, or something else, means. Put in another way, the music for the B flat clarinet, for example, has to be written out a tone higher to get the required sounds. This is not really as difficult as the matter of the international date-line or summer time! Now, if the key of the passage is D minor (one flat), it is clear that a part for B flat clarinet would be written with one sharp, whereas a part for A clarinet would be in four flats; and one sharp is easier than four flats, so why does Elgar choose the latter instrument?

7.   We may as well consider in order the various arguments which might be brought forward.

(a) It might be because the composer wants to use the bottom C sharp—the A clarinet goes down a semitone lower than the B flat clarinet though the bottom note in each case is *written* as E. An investigation of the whole Prelude shows that this is not the case and at the end of the Prelude the clarinets change to B flat.

(b) Let us try now the theory that the composer is going to change key. It certainly proves true that a substantial part of the Prelude is in D Major, which gives the clarinets in A the signature of only one flat. But this argument is not wholly convincing, so we try

(c) Perhaps the composer prefers the warm tone of the A clarinet in its lowest register. Players will tell you that the tone is superior to the B flat. This seems to be the answer.

So the choice of instrument is not a simple matter, but one in which knowledge and loving care are joined to expediency. This is not to say that the B flat clarinet is not 'warm' in its chalumeau register. A beautiful blending of such low notes with divided violas is to be found in Weber's Concertino for clarinet and orchestra, Op. 26 (1811) in the 'più lento' section, just before the final 'allegro'.

8. But it is not clarinets alone that are playing. We have also in the present passage two bassoons. Unlike the clarinets, these bass double reed instruments are playing in their upper register, producing a characteristic thin pinched tone which is like a wash of colour added. Being played by the similar process of blowing, though in a slightly different way, the passage is phrased the same as for the clarinets. Although sometimes used for 'weird' effects[1] or to suggest 'senile mockery', the bassoons are

---

[1] e.g. Dukas, *L'Apprenti Sorcier*.

often considered the jokers of the orchestral pack; yet always with Elgar there is solemn royalty to them. (See also below, paragraph 11.)

9. Then we see that violas are to play with the wood-wind instruments. Here there are several things to notice:

(a) The viola part is written in the alto clef (except for the higher notes which would be in the treble clef). If not already familiar with it, the reader should practise at the piano, or with his voice, such parts, until he is as fluent in reading this clef as treble or bass.

(b) A most important difference between strings and wind is that the curved lines, slurs, indicate phrasing to the latter but *bowing* to the former and although the blower may be sound in wind and limb, the strong arm of the string player is limited in length. So, although string music can *sound* more continuous than wind music, because it is not dependent on breathing, the phrase-marks, indicating reversal of the direction of the bow, are always shorter, as can be seen here.

(c) The actual direction of the bow is important. A pulling bow, marked ⊓ and called a down bow, can produce a good accented effect and is in general used on the first beat of a bar. It may then be asked why the first note here is marked V, which means a pushing, or up, bow. Elgar's meticulous marking here is so that he shall have a down bow at the beginning of bars 2, 3 and 4. Also he does not want too vigorous an opening. In the second bar a note is repeated and the bow is reversed. This is of course intentional, but it may be pointed out that a characteristic string style can be got with a phrase-mark over repeated notes. This would indicate a stopping of the bow while proceeding in the same direction. Look at the last movement of Sibelius's Violin Concerto. After studying the direction of the bow during the soloist's

21

opening bars, turn to the accompanying strings at the second subject at figure **2**. Here repeated notes even have rests between them and yet slurs over them. This is real bowing and much could be gained by getting a string player to demonstrate these points. An even more legato effect is got by the use of a slur together with lines: Here the bow proceeds evenly in the same direction and does not stop, but it is pressed down on the string to make accents where indicated by the lines— another effect unheard-of by the pianist.

(d) Then the fingering is marked. Although not all composers do this, it it not here just a form of spoon-feeding for the player! In the present instance it is a clear indication that the passage is to be played on the C string (this should be thoughtfully followed through by non-string-players). The tone of the lowest string of the viola has a full quality which the composer asks for by putting in the fingering. He could alternatively have written 'sul C' and drawn a line to show for how long. Otherwise the passage would have been played largely on the weaker G string.

(e) 'Con sordino' means with a mute, an appliance fixed to the bridge, which produces a muffled, whispering effect. Here then is the complicated blend of tone-colours applied to a 'unison' passage, which must be listened to with a critical ear, picking out the constituent colours.

10. The important thing to realize is not to write an 'abstract' tune and then say that any instrument with the right compass can tackle it. It is well to get into the habit of thinking of the instruments together with the tunes. The tune must sound as if it was made for the instrument and any limitations must be made into virtues. On rare occasions the abstract thought of the composer is powerful enough to survive a lack of direc-

tion in instrumentation. The Brahms Piano Quintet in F minor, Op. 34, survives, though the composer could not make up his mind whether to write for string quartet, for two pianos, or for one piano with string quartet. And Schumann's Andante and Variations for two pianos, Op. 46, is so full of inspiration that it matters very little whether the actual writing is ideally suited for the instruments or not. What the student might do with profit is to try and find out where the original parts for two cellos and horn fitted in.

Now look back for a moment at Example 1, and imagine the chord an octave lower. Think out the effect on voices and horns, noting that the 'strain' has been eliminated. Think of the string instruments and imagine which strings are to be used. Should the viola play G as an open string? If so it will stand out as rather cold and glaring. This may be effective fortissimo but not so good piano, unless you want it to stand out (observe the open G on the violins in Wagner's Introduction to Act III of *Tristan*). Which note will stand out in the wood-wind ensemble? Although the clarinet is now sounding in the rich and sonorous part of its compass it will not be the first sound to hit the ear. The flute will sound rather weak and 'puffy' so low; the bassoon will be full and robust; but again it will be the oboe which will strike the attention—indeed, with a less-than-expert player it will sound harsh, rough, somewhat explosive. With the *oboe* there is the least amount of variation in prominence; with the *flute* there is the maximum amount of variation but it must be realized that, in this case, it is somewhat controlled; i.e. the lower the flute goes the softer, and the higher it goes the louder it gets. All notes above the stave are impossible to play really softly on the flute and after a few ledger lines they really screech. The oboe and

23

flute (at all levels) are difficult to substitute. You can discreetly alter or omit a middle register note on clarinet or bassoon and have it played by something else but you cannot alter the oboe to something else without a loss of its characteristic quality and you cannot write the *upper* notes of the flute for anything else because of their shrillness. This shrillness can be eliminated by transcribing the passage for piccolo (in which the quality and nuance will match that of a flute playing an octave lower). Look at Verdi's Overture to *La Forza del Destino* at the beginning of the last section (letter **N**) where the piccolo 'points' the high violin notes, pianissimo, itself playing in its lowest register. This characteristic of variation of intensity can be easily judged by doing a little whistling. The human whistling range is not so large as that of the piccolo but its lowest extremity closely resembles that of the piccolo both in pitch and volume.

The nearest substitute for the lower octave of the oboe often has to be the bassoon, but this is more an intellectual self-deception than anything else. It is said—as an excuse —that both have double reeds, but in truth the tone is not very similar (see paragraph 8 above). The violin is sometimes better than nothing.

11. Just as the flute has the limitation of getting louder as it gets higher, so the bassoon is liable to get embarrassingly prominent as it gets lower. It should be remembered that the notes from low F downwards are all obtained by keys as extensions to the natural scale of the instrument and are not too easy to produce with fluency. A bassoonist has a very large selection of keys to control with no more than the usual allocation of fingers and thumbs. Conductors have often thought of altering the bassoon part in Tchaikovsky's Sixth Symphony, in the first movement just before the sudden ferocious 'allegro

vivo' (11 bars before **H**)[1]. As the bassoon part flows straight out of a clarinet passage, the idea of substituting bass clarinet is largely a matter of matching timbre. It might be observed that at this point the composer marks the part with nothing less than *pppppp*, often considered to be an indication of his neuroticism, but to the present writer it can be translated simply, 'Play *softly*, you—son of a—!' However, what the conductors and arrangers have *not* tampered with is the opening of the symphony. Many times the lack of balance here must have struck the listener. It is a passage for bassoon solo accompanied by divided double basses, a magnificently sombre conception, and yet all parts are marked the same *pp*. The result in almost every performance is that the double basses start with a whisper and then a rather coarse bassoon shatters the illusion by entering too prominently. It would certainly be taking a liberty to get this played on the bass clarinet and the only answers to the problem seem to be (a) to make the basses play louder or (b) to ask the broadcasting or recording engineer to 'control' the bassoon with a special microphone!

12. *Score-reading practice.* Start with some of Haydn's string quartets and then some of the smaller orchestral scores of that period.[2] Most of these will be in the form of miniature scores, but bigger editions are available, e.g. the O.U.P. publish the Boyce symphonies (edited by Constant Lambert), which are good for our purpose. There is not much transposition in these, but the viola clef can be learned. Older editions of vocal works may be sight-read to acquire C-clef flexibility and ordinary

[1] See Forsyth, *Orchestration*, p. 278.

[2] See also *The Amateur Orchestra*, Leonard Duck (Appendix II), in this series.

vocal scores can be used for normal four-part reading. Organ-music played at the piano exercises the mind as well as the hands.

13.   *The compass of some instruments.*

    (i) The *written* notes are given first.

    (ii) The arrow indicates that the note is *not* the absolute limit.

    (iii) 8va bassa = an octave lower.

    (iv) The following scheme is useful for indicating notes. The style of lettering is used from each C upwards to the B above it. It saves space here, but the student should transcribe these all into staff notation for himself.

Voices:

Pianoforte:

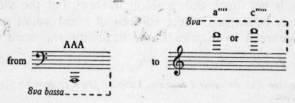

STATICS AND DYNAMICS

Organ:

	Written note		*Stop*

Pedals from   C   sounding:

$$\begin{cases} 16\text{ft.} = \text{CC} \\ 32\text{ft.} = \text{CCC} \\ 64\text{ft.} = \text{CCCC (8 c/s)} \end{cases}$$

to   f′ or g′   sounding

$$\begin{cases} 8\text{ft.} \quad \text{rank}^1 = \text{f′ or g′} \\ 4\text{ft.} \quad \text{rank} = \text{f″ or g″} \end{cases}$$

Manuals   Lowest note as for pedals (8ft. as written)

to   c′′′′   sounding   4ft.   rank¹ = c′′′′′
                                        2ft.   rank = c′′′′′′
                                      ($\frac{3}{4}$ inch. 8Kc/s).

The total range of a large organ may be CCCC to c′′′′′′; and of a normal small organ, CC to c′′′′′.

The usual manuals in order from the highest are

German	*Italian*	*French*	*English*
Brustwerk	D'Espressione	Récit	Swell
Hauptwerk	Principale	Grand Orgue	Great
Unterwerk	di Coro	Positif	Choir

Wood-wind Instruments of the Orchestra:

Flute c′ to c′′′′ ↗

Piccolo d′ to a′′′ ↗ (sounding d″ to a′′′′)

Oboe b♭ to g′′′ ↙

Cor Anglais b (sounding e) to e′′′ (a″)

Clarinet e to b′′′♭ ↗ ('B flat' sounding d to a′′′)
                              ('A' sounding c♯ to g′′′♯)

Bass Clarinet (in B flat) e to g′′′ (sounding D to f″)

Bassoon BB♭ to b′♭ ↗

Double bassoon BB♭ to e′♭   (sounding BBB♭ to e♭)

---

¹ The stop indicates the length of the *lowest* pipe of the set.

Saxophone b♮ to f‴

Soprano	sounding	a♭ to e‴♭
Alto	„	d♭ to a‴♭
Tenor	„	A♭ to e″♭
Baritone	„	D♭ to a″♭

QUESTIONS AND EXERCISES

1.   Rescore the passage from Holst's *The Planets,* given in Example 2: (a) for instruments of the normal full orchestra, (b) for theatre orchestra (for instrumentation see Chapter I).

2.   Write a chord of (a) C sharp minor, (b) C major and (c) B flat major for 2 cl., bass cl., 2 fag., 4 horns (2 in F and 2 in D), 2 tpts. in D, 2 cornets in A[1], 3 trombones, timp. in B flat, D, and E, and strings. (The trumpets and horns here should play only open notes—see Chapter III, para. 9).

Then compare your working with Berlioz and copy out from the 'Menuet des Follets' (*Faust*) the chords at bars 53, 59 and 103.

3.   Write for wood-wind instruments (2222):—
    (a) Perfect Cadence in G major, *ff*
    (b) Imperfect Cadence in D Minor, *pp*
    (c) Plagal Cadence in F major, *mf*
    (d) Interrupted Cadence in A minor, *ff*

4.   Write a chord of E minor for 5 flutes, 3 oboes and cor anglais, 2 bassoons and double bassoon, 3 trombones, timpani in B and G, bass drum, harp, 2 pianofortes, cellos and double basses.

Then compare your working with Stravinsky (the opening chord of the *Symphony of Psalms,* 1930).

5.   Write a chord of G (a fourth lower than the chord in Example 1) both forte and piano for (a) string quartet, (b) voices, (c) 4 horns, (d) fl, ob, cl., fag, (e) vary the spacing of the latter to bring out the tone of the flute *or* the bassoon.

6.

EXAMPLE 5

Couperin, *La Passacaille* (for clavecin, i.e. harpischord), 1716.

[1] Cornets may be treated like modern trumpets.

(a) Phrase this for the keyboard in accordance with Couperin's fingering[1].

(b) Using two staves, and noting especially the *accidentals* in the lower part, write out for two violins with bowing so that bars 2 and 4 have the same direction of bow (for practice indicate on which strings the instruments are to play—nothing out of the ordinary is needed).

(c) Write, with phrasing, for two clarinets, deciding whether to use the B flat or A instrument.

7.

EXAMPLE 6
Glinka, *Kamarinskaia*, 1848

Phrase this (a) for clarinet solo (transposing it) and (b) for violin solo, in accordance with its character.

(c) Transposing down an octave and using the correct clef, rewrite for bassoon.

(d) Harmonize with simple chords for piano.

8. Noting especially the necessity for writing-in one more vital accidental, transcribe for piano the first two bars of the last movement (Adagio lamentoso) of Tchaikovsky's Sixth Symphony.

[1] See *François Couperin and the French Classical Tradition* by Wilfrid Mellers (Dobson, 1950).

III

HARMONY

1. We are going to consider 'harmony' in some detail not only because it is in itself a vital matter—the word being used synonymously with 'music' not only by poets and laymen but frequently by musicians themselves—but because of its constant application to problems of orchestration. Truly the harmony and the colour of a piece can scarcely be separated and this chapter is not at all in the nature of a digression.

2. Before we go into these implications fully, it will be well to consider a few practical points when attempting to transform a piano piece into an orchestral piece. First, then, the actual *writing*, i.e. the layout of notes, tails and groupings, etc. Or are you going to be slovenly and place your notes as if they were bird-limes on wires? If so, you will seriously prejudice performances. It goes without saying that things which are cramped on two staves can be more neatly expressed on single staves for each instrument.

If Exercises 6 and 8 at the end of Chapter II have been successfully negotiated, it will have become obvious

31

that pitfalls can lie in wait for the transcriber who is not meticulously careful about his accidentals. Occasionally a part is better written with enharmonic changes. If, for example, a piece is in B major and a few isolated A sharps are given to the horn in the middle, these notes when written for horn in F may well look best on the part as F rather than as E sharp. The context and the comfort of the player must be balanced against each other in order to decide.

3. When cross-rhythm and syncopations are involved, composers have a habit, when writing for keyboard, of writing 'across the bar-line'. Look, for example, at the last movement, Rondo, of Beethoven's Piano Sonata, Op. 10 No. 3, in D, and observe the phrasing he has used.

Now imagine that you have arranged the opening for strings. What would be your feelings as a cellist were you to see (bar 5):

EXAMPLE 7
Beethoven, Sonata Op. 10 No. 3, last movement

Would you not feel a little happier if the grouping, which Beethoven used for a single instrument, were changed as follows?

EXAMPLE 8

32

(The actual phrasing, which, you will remember, *now* means bowing, has not been altered, though it might have been.)

In my *Pensieri* for string orchestra, I have written one passage for the violins (with syncopated bowing) in the following way:

EXAMPLE 9
Ian Parrott, *Pensieri,* 1950

This *could* have been written (and would have had the same effect):

EXAMPLE 10

but I felt it was easier, in a time like 5/4, the first way, since the subdivision of the bar into two parts was clearer.

4. A reference was made in the last chapter to the vagueness which the sustaining pedal can give to a passage. More important, of course, is the sustaining of harmonies. Some music, using broken chords, sounds 'warm' if the pedal is judiciously used without blurring, but would be decidedly 'cold' or 'bare' if transcribed for orchestra without paying attention to the pedal effect.

Take, by way of example, the following tag (a) and for a moment consider the *wrong* way of transcribing it (b). Each reader will, of course, say that *he* would never dream of doing anything like this, but I would not always be so sure!

33

C

(a)

(b)
bad

EXAMPLE 11

This violates some of the principles already referred to (I *have* actually written the tails the right way up): from the point of view of the comfort of the player, the oboe part would be preposterous played slowly and well-nigh impossible to play fast. And the reader will doubtless remember from the last chapter what I said there about the problem of tone-quality: treated in the manner in which I have scored Example 11(b) there is little doubt that the oboe would sound more like the quacking of an angry duck than anything more musical.

A simple method of treating this problem might very well be:

34

EXAMPLE 12

(Two or more parts may here be compressed on to one stave to save space. The student should *not* do this in his own exercises, except in the case of cello and double bass.)

Several points which should be noted: you will see that the oboe is given the lower notes of the triads instead of the middle ones in this instance;[1] the violins are bowed (and an orchestral abbreviation is used) and it is assumed that the pizzicato bass will have a certain carrying-power and dying-away effect which will aptly convey the impression of the keyboard bass-line. This effect would not be spoilt in any way by adding *sustained* notes (dotted minim followed by dotted crotchet) for bassoon which would sound 'behind' the string bass.

If you are wondering what to do with the second violins and violas, who are sitting there twiddling their thumbs, then you can give them some harmony notes while carefully making sure that the string parts are *in themselves* complete:

[1] If a quiet effect is wanted, the oboe should not be used at all.

EXAMPLE 13

5. Note that the second violin part should not, without special reason, go above the first violin line, particularly if it obscures the outline of the original. Here the weak pizzicato tone of the second violin E will not stop one hearing clearly the first violin's opening C—though Heaven knows we have little to lose in the present somewhat banal exercise. If people cannot recognize the original then far too much monkeying must have been in evidence! Never monkey and never say, 'Have you heard *my* version of Bach, Beethoven, etc.?' The time signature has been changed, since it will be easier, if this sort of writing is to continue (the cello and double bass line should be similarly altered). In broken harmony, where possible consider the harmony notes as going to the equivalent note in the following group, i.e. the first to the first, the second to the second and the third to the third.

Have a look at Bach's Prelude in D minor in the first book of the '48'. Although the pedal was not used, since the composer would have played this on the delicately whispering clavichord, this prelude can be treated similarly to our Example 11(a) by adding a back-wash of wood-wind as shown in Example 12. Incidentally the speed of performance is generally assumed to be pretty fast and one wonders what would happen after a few bars

equivalent to Example 11(b)! It is worth playing through
this prelude, slowly, stressing on one occasion all the
second notes of the triplets and on another all the *third*
notes. This is not meant to be a public performance—if
you did that sort of thing in public, you would be removed
bodily from the platform after a few ripe tomatoes had
reached their target—but just for your own amusement
and to discover the hidden melodies which lie concealed
amongst Bach's notes in ordered sequence.

6. One more use of the sustaining pedal, before we go
on to harmony proper. Consider things the other way
round and imagine you are transferring a short loud chord
for orchestra to the piano.

(a) Do not forget what was said above about limits.
The same note should, of course, be at the bottom, but
so should the top note be at the top—with the qualifying
clause that if the flute had a note slightly higher than the
more powerful violins, the impression might still be of the
violins being at the top.

(b) Space the other notes so that they lie under the two
hands comfortably.

(c) An important point, not always realized, is that the
orchestra has a sustaining effect. It may be quite a time,
according to the acoustics of the hall—no time in the
Royal Festival Hall—before the reverberation of a
staccato chord dies away. Obviously this can easily be
suggested on the pianoforte by a touch of the pedal. All
these points can be studied by looking at the first page of
Beethoven's Eroica Symphony and comparing with it
Liszt's transcription for pianoforte.

7. Now let us see where you've forgotten your harmony!

Take the following melody and harmonize it as simply
as possible—merely sketching the chords you propose
to use.

EXAMPLE 14

Have you done that? (Ten minute interval.)

Now let me have a look at what you've done.

I said 'as *simply* as possible'—look at all these chords!
Why do so many of you, I wonder, assume that (a) you
must harmonize every note that is jumped at with a
different chord and (b) a chromatic note means a modulation and (c) the tonic or dominant chords must be avoided
like the plague? And (d) why have you harmonized the
last three notes (D C B) as V to I? This is not a cadence,
you know—not this way at any rate, even if your mind *is*
running on polonaises (where the accents are reversed)
and this is not a polonaise. Surely a cadence is normally
weak to strong. Goodness gracious, etc.!

I think we shall have to straighten out a few points in
elementary harmony before we can apply our knowledge
to the orchestra. Let us first see if we cannot assess the
formal shape of this extract—it is, after all, a piece of
formalized eighteenth century writing. If that is so, we
can divide it into two sections, not only as regards the
melodic shape but as regards the harmony:

	a.			b.		
melody notes	G		C	A		B
chords	I		V7	V		I

EXAMPLE 15

If you study this plan carefully some of you will be staggered perhaps to observe that the *only* chords suggested are tonic and dominant! Yes, I goes to V in the first half; and then the neat answer is V going to I in the second half. The tune actually *suggests* that, if you study it carefully. Perhaps it was the third bar which was puzzling. You may have wondered how D sharp and E could be part of the dominant chord? Well, the D sharp is a chromatic passing note to E which is a dominant ninth. Those people who imagined that dominant ninths formed no part of the vocabulary of Haydn and Mozart will have to think again. The last note of this bar, the C, is a dominant seventh. Ah, but this note does not resolve by going down, you say. You mean it doesn't go down *immediately*. No, but the intervening notes are ornamental. Another surprise is in store. The final B is really the answer (or resolution) to the C that occurs right back on the second crotchet of bar 2; in other words, the last note of phrase 'a' is matched by the last note of phrase 'b'. It is matched at the appropriate point in the bar. (Compare on a much speedier scale, the Bach prelude triplets, para. 5 above.)

8. This may have seemed an unnecessary preliminary to some students, but it must be emphasized that if the harmonic plan is incorrect, no amount of orchestral jugglery will cover the fault. The next stage, of course, is to write something which gets away from the ponderous hymn-like flavour of our sketch. Several things which can be done may include passing or auxiliary notes of various types, but one of the most powerful devices for lightening the texture will be the use of rests. You could simply write your chords as crotchets at the beginning of bars. More subtle than that, you could write the rests first. So long as the mind is properly satisfied as to the

39

harmonic framework, according to a plan, the first melody-notes of bars will not sound up-in-the-air. Now prepare something not too heavy with regard to instruments and see what you can do.

I wonder if you have done anything like this:

EXAMPLE 16
Mozart, *Don Giovanni*, Finale, 1788

At the end of the above passage, after a light and airy string accompaniment, Mozart introduces two flutes and two bassoons in octaves, a characteristic device. He also introduces the horns, which, since this is the tonic chord, play most naturally the keynote.

9.   A few words about the sort of horns that Mozart had to write for would not be untimely here. 'Natural' horns, like hunting horns, military bugles and other brass instru-

40

ments relied entirely on differing lip pressure to get a change of note. Thanks to the harmonic series,[1] in a composition in the major key all the brass instruments could at least play all the notes of the tonic chord, if suitably placed. This was done by slipping in a brass coil (called a crook) of the requisite size before the piece started. Some of these players had to carry quite a bag of crooks about with them. If a composition in the minor key had to be tackled it was not so easy, as the minor third was unobtainable except very high up and even then the mouthpiece had to be suitably constructed. No amount of cunning lip work would get a wanted minor third on a bugle—though one might come out by accident. On the other hand the conical French horn mouthpiece, unlike the cup-shaped one of the other brass instruments, favours the upper partials.

It is interesting to see what Mozart does in his G minor Symphony (K.550). He uses two horns, one with a G crook and one with a high B flat crook. Those who know a little about sonata form can readily guess how the horns' work is divided. Which horn, for example, in the first and last movements, has most to do at the end of the exposition, and which at the end of the recapitulation? It is suggested that the student goes through these, noting the 'statutory' modulation to the relative major and the parcelling out of notes to these instruments, particularly comparing, in the Finale, the last eight bars of the exposition with the last eight bars of the whole work. Make a composite list first of all of the notes made available by the use of the two crooks. In Beethoven the question of modulation often appears one of the whim of the moment—and tremendous skill in the handling of his brass is always evident, as, for example,

[1] See below, para. 13.

in the Fifth Symphony. In the first movement the horns have a magnificent solo phrase in the exposition at bars 59-62. What happens later? Why, the bassoons play it (see para. 10 of Chapter II for the remark about 'limitations made into virtues'). The uninstructed audience say in effect, 'What a pleasant change of tone colour!' But we, who know the bald truth that the horns do not play it simply because they cannot, are none the less delighted by the change.

Turn on now to the slow movement: this is surely remarkable. The key is A flat and yet the brass instruments are in C! Study it and you will see that here then is a case of the composer making this apparent nuisance into one of the most flashing facets of the structure— the whole thing is intimately bound up with the composer's creative thought. Since those days, with the invention of valves, horns have played a complete chromatic scale with comparative ease. Great as is this overall gain, no composer has ever again been in a position to incorporate into his score such an electrifying colour-form effect even if he wanted to, not even Berlioz. In his preface to *Tristan*, Wagner wrote as follows: 'Owing to the introduction of valves, the gain to this instrument has been so great that it is impossible to ignore these accessories, although the horn thereby has undoubtedly lost some of its beauty of tone . . .' Valves have, however, come to stay, and it has been partly music of *Tristanesque* difficulty which has made them indispensable. It should be observed, however, that no one preserved the character of the horn more faithfully than did Wagner himself, and in Act II, Scene 1, he employs behind the stage six additional horns to represent the sounds of a hunt and these horns play only the open notes of the 'natural' instrument!

42

Different crooks were used in earlier music and it became customary to continue 'pairing' the players even with the new instruments. Horns should still be written for as pairs of 'high' and 'low': with four horns it is assumed that the first and third players are specialists in high notes and the second and fourth are those who keep their lip technique for the lower notes. Holst (in Example 2) has preserved the pattern, though he might have interchanged horns II and IV, making a more complete dovetailing.

10. We have already dealt a little with 'blending'. The horn is often kept in a separate orchestral pigeon-hole from the other brass, because it so frequently blends better with other groups, particularly the wood-wind.[1] In Walton's Symphony, the combination of stopped horn notes (*chiuso*) and strings *sul pont.* in the scherzo does a good deal to bring out the mood of *malizia* which the composer wants.

A few words should now be given about the general blend of brass instruments. We had better glance back at the scheme given in Chapter I and add on either side of our 'Theatre' and our 'Symphony' orchestras, the 'Small' and the 'Wagnerian' orchestras. In brief, the smaller the orchestra the subtler has to be the blending. A small orchestra, for example, might have one trumpet and one trombone; if they can rub shoulders with one horn, then that will complete our brass section: three very different types of instrument to listen to. The trumpet and trombone will stand out more and more the louder the music grows and in forte passages the horn will lack the brilliant 'edge' of the other two, even when playing high in its compass. It is, we must remember, the sound, not the

[1] Wagner often places it among the wood-wind in his scores, but generally the student should not do this.

43

metal, which is the criterion of blending. But we need not let this restrict us to three-part harmony. Two very good *filling-in* instruments, if carefully written for, are the bassoon to go with the horn and the clarinet to act as a companion to the trumpet, preferably playing as a 'second' or lower part. If you avoid the lowest register of the clarinet (which is too richly reedy), this instrument in its middle register will make a good alto line to a trumpet melody if not too loud.The bassoons will also blend well with trombones if the latter are playing *softly*. There are some good examples of this in Schubert's *Lazarus*. Schubert, incidentally, is fond of using a single trombone as bass to the wood-wind (see the slow movement of the 'Great' C major Symphony, middle section), or to re-inforce the general bass (see, for example, here and there in the 'Unfinished' Symphony). In all blending exercises it is important to dovetail where necessary to smooth out the very real differences that are there. Also all increases and decreases of volume of sound must be attended to. We have already noted the characteristics of some wood-wind instruments in this respect. In the case of the brass, a mental picture should be ever present of the loose lip and quiet notes at the bottom of the compass and the tight lip, strained impression and loud tone of the top notes. A brass instrument should be allowed to 'warm up' by starting off easily somewhere in the middle. The roof-raising effect of the top notes (after preliminary warming) is exploited in the show-piece *Iron Foundry* (*Music of Machines*) composed in 1928 by Mossolov. He knows that the horns will make a devil of a row if all four of them are expected to play up to top B flat. So—to be hanged for a sheep as for a lamb—he actually asks the players not only to point the bells of their instruments upwards—which he says in French—but also to stand up while they play, which he directs in Russian and German.

11. To compare the two extremes in size of orchestra, it is instructive to look at both *Siegfried* and the *Siegfried Idyll*. In the former complete uniformity of tone-colour is possible in four-part chords by the use of quartets of instruments: in each team a bass (or semi-bass) is provided for each group except the flutes;[1] i.e. the cor anglais goes with three oboes and the bass-clarinet with three clarinets, etc. It is interesting to note that the trombones, separated from the trumpets, are a group to themselves; the trumpets have their own bass (an instrument now obsolete) and the tubas are a complete set to themselves. This does not, however, prevent Wagner from blending instruments from different groups with very great skill. He also makes much of the difference between one instrument and two playing in unison—leading to the 'secondary-colour' type of writing which we observe in Elgar (see Example 3). The main difference with the *Idyll* is, of course, that there the composer cannot luxuriate in masses of uniform timbre or in much doubling, but is confined all the time to the blending of heterogeneous elements—which also has its unlimited possibilities.

12. *Score-reading practice*.

Continuing from the work prescribed at the end of the last chapter, more eighteenth-century orchestral scores should be tackled, the clarinets, horns and trumpets all being quickly and fluently transposed. Try to transpose by thinking of the *key*. Fanfare-like passages for the brass should be read in terms of tonic and dominant, etc., a complete phrase being mentally absorbed; avoid, if possible, transposing note by note. Become accustomed to Bach and Handel scores with trumpets in D (e.g. *The*

---

[1] It was left to Holst to popularize the bass flute in *The Planets*.

Christmas Oratorio and *Messiah*), then have a look at Mozart's fond treatment of the clarinet. Practise crossing parts without necessarily crossing the hands. Work at Morley's two-part canzonets and Purcell's three-part fantasias for example.

When a large score is being read at the piano, the player has to learn quite unashamedly to 'fake'—but there is good faking and bad. Speedily it has to be decided which parts must be only suggested or even left out altogether. It is possible to play less than fifty per cent of the total notes written and yet to play ninety-nine per cent of the component notes of each harmony. A general impression must be given, making sure that all essential notes in the texture are as far as possible played. Some of the inner parts may be put down or up an octave in order that they shall lie easily under the hands and so that confusion of line shall be avoided. All the works mentioned in this chapter can be studied in this way partly at the keyboard. If any parts are to be left out, try to see that it is not always the clarinet or horn which is overlooked, otherwise it might be suspected that you are shirking your responsibility!

13. *The Harmonic Series.*

A knowledge of this subject is necessary to a full understanding of the basic or 'natural' notes of the brass instruments and also harmonics on the strings.

If you take a given note as a starting point and double its number of vibrations per second and then treble, quadruple and so on as many times as you wish, you form not a scale but a 'harmonic' series of notes, the intervals between which become smaller and smaller as they get higher. These intervals become progressively dissonant, their mathematical ratios becoming increasingly complex. It will be noticed that the lower six notes form the major

46

common chord; and as the lower harmonics are quite audibly prominent on many instruments, it will be readily understood that the major chord has a greater degree of richness through the sympathetic vibrations of 'overtones' than more complicated chords (of which the minor chord is one). A 50 c/s electric mains will produce a hum in some wireless sets of the second note of the series, approximately G (100 c/s)[1] so we will take this as our starting point.

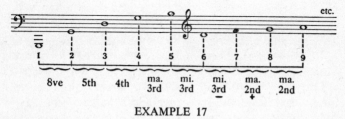

EXAMPLE 17

The f' marked in black is slightly flat. It should be possible to hear this and most of those harmonics below it if the fundamental GG is struck and sustained on the piano.

The continuation of the series should be plotted by the student up to the 16th harmonic, by doubling the figures already given. Thus 10 is b' (twice 5). The intervening notes can then be plotted (i.e. 11, 13, 15) and it will be observed that these make the succession roughly scale-wise at this level. Other notes can of course be chosen as fundamentals to produce different series and in the case of the brass instruments of the orchestra it is useful to think of the basic series of each (the fundamental is generally not obtainable so the series starts with harmonic No. 2).

[1] Higher harmonics can sometimes be heard in electric fires, etc.

Trumpet in B flat

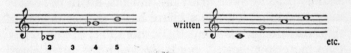

EXAMPLE 18a

By pulling out a slide, most modern trumpets can be 'put into A', a semitone lower.

Horn in F[1]

EXAMPLE 18b

On valve instruments, the valves lower the series by a tone, a semitone and by a tone and a half respectively.

Tenor Trombone—The series is based on BB flat.

Bass Trombone—The series is based on GG.

In the case of the former a satisfactory fundamental (called a pedal note) is obtainable. On the latter, as in the case of the mains hum, it is not. By use of the slide, seven different *series* of notes are obtainable. These instruments are *non-transposing,* i.e. you write the actual notes as sounded. Each position of the slide lowers the whole series by a semitone. Thus the seventh position of the *bass* trombone gives the series based on CC sharp; and C sharp is actually the bottom note of this instrument (there are no satisfactory pedal notes). The pedal notes are obtainable on the *tenor* trombone down to the third position, thus giving AA flat as the bottom note of this instrument. The student should now discover for himself

---

[1] In the time of Beethoven, horn notes in the bass clef were written an octave too low. Also high notes for the cello in the treble clef were written an octave too high. This is not now done.

why the instrument has *not* got a complete chromatic compass and, in fact, why there is a 'gap' of unobtainable notes between BB flat and E. Also it should be borne in mind that the pedal notes need some preparation on the part of the player and sound rather coarse. The trombones play with ease up to the 8th harmonic and these notes in first position give a good guide to the top notes to write in normal orchestral work. Example 17 can be adapted to visualize all the notes, except the lowest, available on a bass trombone without moving the arm from first position. The trombone is the only instrument, apart from percussion, which requires no fingers—and it is now seen that it doesn't always need physical jerks either. For obvious reasons, do not write legato passages too low down.

Looking back on the valve instruments for a moment, imagine you wish to play a chromatic scale downwards. What you do is to press down valves in various combinations as follows: 2, 1, 1 + 2[1], 2 + 3, 1 + 3, 1 + 2 + 3. This would be necessary if, for instance, you are playing on a B flat trumpet and wanted to descend from f' to b. To go down one further semitone, you would release all the valves and loosen the lip (thus altering the 'embouchure' to pitch the next note in the natural series. It is interesting to observe that the valves act in the same way as the slide on the trombone, giving *seven* positions, which are sufficient to give a complete chromatic scale.

Tuba. This is a valve instrument, but because of the great gap from the second harmonic down to the fundamental (which on the modern orchestral instrument is FF) it has a fourth valve. It is non-transposing. It blends properly with neither horns nor trombones, its best

[1] *Not* 3, which gives wrong intonation on its own.

49

D

function being, in loudish passages, to strengthen the bass line of the full orchestra.

Brass instruments can be written for safely up to the 8th harmonic. Exceptionally, the horns (see para. 9), can be taken up to the 12th easily and, in virtuoso writing (see Chapter 2, para. 2) up to the 16th. This is because of the different shaped mouthpiece. It is better for the student to think this out for himself rather than blindly to consult a table, so in consequence the compass of brass instruments is *not* summarized in this book.

QUESTIONS AND EXERCISES

1.   Continue with Example 12 for at least eight bars adding a melody on some other instruments, starting with a horn solo.

2.   (a) Write out the harmonic series for the tenor trombone in 3rd position up to the 8th harmonic. Include the pedal note.

(b) Show how many alternative ways there are of producing f′ and say in which position it would be least satisfactory (tenor trombone), and why?

3.   (a) Write the chord of Example 1 for two trumpets in A and two trombones. (NB. The tenor trombone should be in the tenor clef.)

(b) Write for brass, 0331: Perfect Cadence in G mi. *ff*, and Plagal Cadence in B mi. *pp*. (NB.—You should avoid consecutive fifths. If a part is doubled in octaves the two instruments should preferably be dissimilar.)

4.   Score the opening nine bars of Beethoven's Piano Sonata, Op. 27 No. 2 (the 'Moonlight') for full orchestra. (Para. 5.)

5.   (a) Harmonize the following, using only I, V and a single, well-placed, example of II (V may be with the seventh).

(b) Using your own harmonic basis as above, write an accompaniment for keyboard[1] with elaborate figuration.

(c) Based again on the above, write an accompaniment for wood-wind, two horns and strings.

Then compare your working with:

EXAMPLE 19
Mozart, *The Magic Flute*, 1791

[1] Pianoforte or glockenspiel.

6.   Rearrange the following to make correct individual instrumental parts with suitable phrasing (i.e. noting the progression of the parts, which is not necessarily clear—in keyboard writing, the notes are often written simply to lie under the fingers) and score for cl., fag., 2 horns, va., vcl. and cb.

EXAMPLE 20

Schumann, *Album for the Young, Winter Time II*, Op. 68 No. 39, 1848

7.   (a) Study the final chords of Tchaikovsky's Fantasy-Overture, *Romeo and Juliet*, bars 493-507 (i.e. ten bars after the beginning of the final 'moderato assai') and estimate which instruments will be most prominent and which will not. Then listen to a gramophone recording of the passage and check your findings.

(b) Write a similar passage for 2 fl., 1 ob., cor. a., 2 cl., 2 fag. and 2 horns.

8.   (a) Arrange for pianoforte the opening six and a half bars of the first movement of Beethoven's Seventh Symphony (para. 6).

(b) Explain why the horns are in D in the third movement (*presto*), which is in the key of F.

9.   (a) Arrange for pianoforte the trio of the third move-

ment of Mozart's Symphony in E flat (1788), K.549. Indicate *three* ways in which the echo effects of the flute may be reproduced and say why *one of* them is unsatisfactory.

(b) Look at the beginning of the movement proper (the Menuetto) and estimate whether the low notes of the violins in bar 2 will be heard above the din of the full wind. What should the conductor do in performance with all the first eight bars? (Get your local amateur orchestra to play it, and listen.)

10.

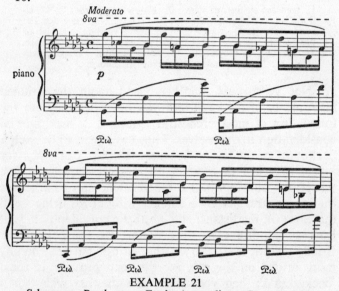

EXAMPLE 21

Schumann, *Posthumous Etudes* (appendix to Op. 13), 1834

(a) Find all the hidden melodies (revise para. 5).

(b) *Precede* the above two bars by a bar of similar decoration on the tonic chord alone. *Follow* the extract by a bar in which a modulation is made to the dominant.

(c) Add a further four bars, making eight bars in all, to round off the piece.

(d) Transposing the whole into an easier key, arrange for orchestra: 2221, 4230, Timp., Str.

IV

INSTRUMENTAL RESOURCE

1. General string qualities. 2. Fingering chords. 3. Positions on the violin. 4. Application. 5. Balance for the conductor. 6. Overlap. 7. Imaginative reading. 8. Use of percussion. 9. Use of available resource. 10. Vocal score. 11. Method in rehearsal. 12. Score-reading. 13. Compass of percussion and string instruments.

1. Not very much has been said about the stringed instruments of the orchestra yet, but since they are the foundation of most orchestral writing they need special consideration in themselves. They have been made such a backbone or mainstay because (a) they can play for longer stretches than wind instruments (bowing is less tiring than blowing) and (b) their sound can be accepted for longer stretches by a listener without *his* tiring—and the effect on the listener, the aesthetic consideration, is at least as important as the comfort of the performers. Briefly then, it is true to say that strings can be generally more restful on the ear, i.e. they can provide an ideal 'background'; their vocabulary is somewhat wider; their powers of difficult execution on the whole greater; and (as can be shown by comparing with the discussion of wood-wind instruments in Chapter II and of brass instruments in Chapter III) their command of *nuance* and *sostenuto* is unrivalled; in the one, they can range with the utmost control from loud to soft in any part of their compasses (with the possible exception of the lowest part of the cello and double bass, which is liable to be sub-

54

dued); and as regards the other, their power to sustain long notes unflinchingly (if need be, the direction of the bow can be almost imperceptibly reversed) they can rival all other instruments and can beat keyboard and percussion in particular.

2. Ideally speaking, the writer for the orchestra should obtain *practical* experience of at least one stringed instrument, preferably the violin, as a genuine 'feel' for the strings is well-nigh impossible without it. Double-stopping, for example, can be made reasonably easy for the player without loss of effect. A glance back at Example 13 will demonstrate this basic principle. The notes E and C could have been given to the violin and G to the viola and, in this instance, it would not have been particularly trying to the performer. However, the dovetailing of the parts, as written, *is* easier on the violinist and, if this sort of passage were to be speeded up, there might be a really noticeable difference. Briefly, if the violinist or violist is asked to play a chord of less than a fifth, then one or more fingers will have to be arched over a string, allowing it to vibrate freely underneath; for intervals of a fifth or more, on the other hand, the fingers can lie naturally on the strings, the first finger furthest over and the others each a string back as in chord (a) below:

EXAMPLE 22

Apart from chords using open strings at their lower end, this is one of the easiest (and therefore most effective) chords to write. It should be observed that only two notes can be sustained for any length of time, the full chord being played *arpeggiando,* usually starting from the lowest

55

note. The values of the upper notes should be accurately indicated, while the lower ones can be given black heads (see chord (b) above). Practice should be gained in writing large chords for the strings, bearing in mind that triple and quadruple stopping is best in loud passages. Thick chords in pianoforte pieces should be transcribed for the string orchestra, remembering that chords which lie under the hands in the one will sound better if spaced out more evenly in the other. The characteristic registers of the various string instruments should always be present in the mind. Chords (a) and (b) above may be transposed up by semitones or tones step by step half a dozen times, the player laying his fingers on the instrument as before, not now in 'first position' but in one of the other seven positions (compare with the trombone, Chapter III, para. 13), noting that there are many alternative ways of playing the same note.

3. The hand positions for the violin can be given here for the G string and the reader can work out the notes for the other strings and also for the other instruments. The position of the *hand* moves up by tones and semitones according to the fundamental scale of the string. The *fingers* are moved up or down a semitone to obtain the chromatic alterations.

The lowest, or 'first', finger in 1st pos. plays a, a♭ or a♯

,,	,,	,,	,,	,,	,,	2nd pos. plays b, or b♭ etc.
,,	,,	,,	,,	,,	,,	3rd pos. plays c′, or c′♯
,,	,,	,,	,,	,,	,,	4th pos. plays d′ or d′♭
,,	,,	,,	,,	,,	,,	5th pos. plays e′ or e′♭
,,	,,	,,	,,	,,	,,	6th pos. plays f′ or f′♯
,,	,,	,,	,,	,,	,,	7th pos. plays g′, g′♭ or g′♯

It might be asked why these higher notes should be played on the G string when they are available more easily on a higher string. There are two answers. One is this matter of 'characteristic tone' which was mentioned above. 'The Air on the G String' demonstrates this point (though Bach did not himself write it in this way). There is a rich and full-blooded quality, which is not present on the D string—the same fullness applies to the viola C. The other is of course a matter of ease of execution. Rapid scales and arpeggios must be thought out to suit the fingers. Such a simple chord as the two notes e' and g' might be considered. Will you play the e' on the D string? Well, what will happen to the g' then? You cannot play two notes on the same string, so we suggest e' as the third finger on the G string and g' as first finger on the D string. The hand is in 3rd position. Can you visualize the arching of the third finger over the D string, which is inevitable with a chord of less than a fifth?

All this may seem unimportant to some non-string players, but even a rudimentary knowledge of the mechanics of playing will help the writer for the orchestra and also give a sense of understanding and co-operation to the budding conductor. There is nothing an amateur player likes better than for the conductor to say, 'Here, give me your fiddle a moment. I'll show you what I want' —and nothing more upsetting to the truculent professional who has been about to say, 'I don't believe he can even *play* any instrument'.

4. Here is a passage from *Walküre*. Which instruments are implied by these parts? (Other parts are omitted for the sake of space.) Each line, you will note, is concerned with arpeggios.

The top line can hardly be suggestive of triple-stopping on a stringed instrument after what has been learnt in this chapter. It is more likely to be three separate instruments and the experienced score-reader will quickly sum up the contrast here of the E flat arpeggio when the other

EXAMPLE 23
Wagner, *Walküre*, Siegmund's Love Song, 1854-5

instruments are playing A flat. Quickly the idea of horns in F comes to the mind. See the subtle and suggestive 'natural' effect of the bare arpeggio, even with the seventh at the end on the first horn. The use of notes which remind one of the older instrument is most valuable in preserving the character of the brass. We may, by the way, have an edition of Wagner without any Italian terms so it is as well to know a little German. 'Weich', for example, means 'tender' and the above legato passage would not be so likely to come off on trumpets, even muted. (Note the repeated accidentals for *each* horn.)

5. Now shall we turn to the lower staves? There is a marked contrast here, which shows the essence of good instrumental writing. It is to be hoped that the reader has named the middle instrument as the harp and the lower as the viola. Easy though the former may be to play on the piano, the latter would not be so easy with one hand. But what matters, of course, is 'Is it easy to play on the viola?' There should be no difficulty in assess-

ing how it lies under the fingers when the hand is placed in second position. It is, of course, an application of the lesson learnt from Example 22 and in paragraph 3. This very small quotation is from a passage which is an accompaniment to the tenor voice singing in its middle register. In addition—a fact often overlooked in concert performances—Wagner, in his orchestration, reckons on a pit to mellow the heavier instruments. The student should discover just how 'weich' his local amateur horns can play and also how lightly and easily the violas can sweep across the strings. Of course adjustments can be, and are, made when an operatic aria is transferred to the concert hall. For one thing, the singer is nearest the audience, instead of being farthest away. Yet there are many types of adjustment and the vital matter of balance is one which has to be settled anew at each rehearsal. The young conductor gets over the first self-conscious stage of concentrating on wagging his arms about; then he really listens to the players; he checks them if they drag or if they play out of tune; finally he thinks of them as a painter looking at his colours and settles the blend and balance. Before tackling the blazing colours of a full orchestra, it is profitable to become reasonably expert in spotting correct and incorrect blend and balance in various choirs, both amateur and professional. Following this, the blend and balance in a string quartet should be studied: first, look at the score: take, for example, the fourth movement of Sibelius's String Quartet, *Voces Intimae,* and assess the effect in your mind of the different instruments playing the same tune in different parts of their compass and on different strings. Then listen to a performance (on gramophone, if necessary) and *memorize* the actual tone-qualities so that you will have an aural impression next time you look at such a passage. First the tune is played low on the first violin

in D minor. Now consider this same subject when it
appears in B minor nine bars before figure **5**, distributed
amongst all four players and finally again in D minor in
the last eight bars of the movement; note particularly the
effect of the viola playing the same notes at the same
pitch and also sul G and yet sounding different. The most
brilliant sul G effect occurs, incidentally, just before this
(fifteen bars after figure **8**). All four instruments are playing in unison, the G string tone of the upper three being
combined with the rich penetrating quality of the cello's
A (highest) string. This movement can be studied also for
innumerable details of bowing and expression, which will
benefit the student as conductor, score-reader or composer. The fact that hardly any of this quartet can
be played satisfactorily on the piano is an additional
tribute to the striking string technique displayed throughout.

6. This difference in quality throughout the various
strings has to be considered when writing ordinary extended scale passages—the sort of thing that pianists
ripple up and down with such mixed pleasure for ex-
aminations. Obviously there should be an 'overlap', de-
pending on the speed. For very *fast* scales, the last note
of one instrument should overlap the first of the next;
it can be given the correct value with a dot over it (it is
generally undesirable that one instrument should finish
before the other starts) and, preferably, it should be on
a beat. Here the difference of quality or intensity is
hardly noticeable because of the speed (see example (a)
below). In *slow* scale passages any difference of quality
is immediately noticeable, for example that between a
cello playing high up and a violin in its middle register.
The overlap here can be more extended, as many as three
notes being doubled, and (see example (b) below) it is

very necessary to indicate different nuances, if the 'join' is to be almost imperceptible:

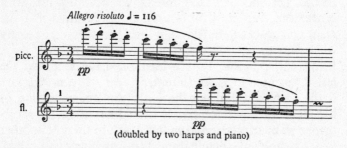

(doubled by two harps and piano)

(other parts omitted)

EXAMPLE 24

Aaron Copland, Symphony 3, (a) fourth movement, (b) third movement, 1944-6

7. The average person (and even an occasional conductor) just does not *read* a score with full details. Plenty of people know the general sound roughly, but may miss the special effect of tone-colour and 'overlap'. For example, the march theme in Wagner's *Meistersinger* overture, which is derived from an old tune of the time of Hans Sachs, sounds continuous, but no single instrument plays it right through. Look at the horns, trumpets and other instruments to see how the notes are allocated to give the resulting sound its shape (see miniature score, bar 40, etc.). The more knowledge of harmony there is, the more likely it is that the reader will quickly assimilate

61

and integrate in his mind all the notes on a score. With his awareness of the harmonic language of a period, he should become in a position to correct misprints with confidence. We must, of course, be forewarned that the great composers were (through their greatness) frequently whimsical disregarders of the conventions of their time. In an earlier book[1] I have mentioned the fact that the last drum note in *A Midsummer Night's Dream* overture is the dominant and not the tonic. An understanding of Mendelssohn's harmonic style should not allow the score-reader to be careless; and in this overture there is another fine example of imagination, transcending the normal, which requires scrupulous reading: the wood-wind chord which interrupts the fairylike rustling of the strings near the beginning. This chord is *not* 'merely' a diminished seventh over a pedal. One of the upper notes is the same as the bass, adding an unusual piquancy to the sound. This is an excellent chord to listen to for balance and also for hearing the unusual note (this has often been transcribed wrongly for piano by those who have jumped too quickly to conclusions)[2] and it should be read first, including its context of exquisite string writing (bar 39 of the score).

If there is a clear understanding of the basic harmony of a piece, the student should have no fears about decoration. Following on the work started in Chapter III, scores should be studied where all forms of unessential note are sounded simultaneously with harmony notes. The effect is never as harsh as on the pianoforte and frequently the clash is non-existent to the ear. Beethoven had a way of making his clashes stand out, but most of the nineteenth-

[1] *A Guide to Musical Thought* (Student's Music Library), Dobson, 1955.

[2] Including the composer?

century writers, in their orchestral writing, achieved a smoothness to the ear while giving perhaps a jagged appearance on paper. The appoggiatura of the fourth falling to the third over a major chord is a bugbear to the harmony beginner, but in orchestral colour the clash of fourth against third is considerably softened and if the instruments are of different types, the clash frequently vanishes. Harmonic clashes count for very little in vocal writing, almost the only effective way of producing heard dissonance being by the time-honoured suspension.

8. Some general advice should be given on the use of percussion instruments. Without going into details about the various capabilities of these instruments (which should of course be studied, preferably by going into the rehearsal room of a large orchestra and getting friendly with the people who play them), it is as well to consider their principal function, which is *accessory*. Even the most 'musical' of them, the timpani, could hardly sustain a whole evening to itself, though in his Sonata for Kettle-drums (1947), Daniel Jones has ingeniously managed, by vital and subtle variety of rhythmic patterns, to keep the interest of the listener throughout four movements in a work which is unaccompanied and which contains only three notes in each movement. Leading professional orchestras today have mechanical timpani on which any notes in the compass can be quickly produced. When writing for standard timpani, however, sufficient time must be given in which to alter the notes. Generally, one can say that percussion instruments (even those with a comparatively large range of definite pitch sounds) can be likened to the use of sequence. The normal unwritten law about exact sequence is that when a figure has been repeated sequentially twice, it then begins to pall. The first

repetition is a necessity to establish its very existence, the second is usually a pleasure but the third tends to sound like a garrulous bore. Much the same psychology applies to the 'accessory' sounds which provide seasoning from the 'kitchen' department of the orchestra. When you have heard one stroke on the triangle, you perhaps feel a need for another, not too soon perhaps, but at a balancing point in the musical structure. After hearing three or four, your palate becomes jaded—you cannot spit it out as in wine-tasting—and the impression may become that of a high-class restaurant, a pier band, or even a low dive, where no one ever listens to the music anyway. This may be general advice, but single, unrepeated notes on gong or bass drum can be extremely effective. Liszt writes a short jingle for *unaccompanied* triangle in his Piano Concerto in E flat. Also an extensive clamour of percussion can frequently be justified—particularly, if one of the vital lessons from the child's percussion band is learnt, i.e. to make use of crescendo and diminuendo. The side drum is very good at this sort of thing. At the end of this chapter, there is an exercise on a piece in which Grieg flagrantly breaks the rule we gave about sequence. The sequential repetitions are shameless and numerous, so much so that they pile up on our numbed senses with a new sort of cumulative excitement. The *cresc.* and *dim.* marked in for the pianist can be worked out in the orchestra by the careful addition and subtraction of instruments, noting especially where the phrases can be said to begin and end for the overlaps. We may as well enjoy ourselves and make a bit of noise with the percussion, too, in the spirit of the original.

Writing for percussion does not always imply noise. The celesta, played by a keyboard, is a quiet instrument, most effective when it has passage-work such as is to be found in Bartók's *Music for Strings, Percussion and Celesta* (1936), for example the end of the first movement. It may be supposed that Bartók, writing here for string orchestra, percussion, harp and piano as well, is presumably including the harp with 'strings', the piano with 'percussion' and the celesta in a separate category of its own.

9. A certain amount was said in Chapter II about substituting one instrument for another. If the most appropriate instrument available has not got the right compass, it might be possible to transpose the whole movement to suit it, just as songs are often put up or down by long-suffering accompanists to suit different singers' vocal ranges and temperamental vagaries. Here is a sort of musical quiz. You have, let us say, three clarinet players in a certain district and it is decided that Stravinsky's *Berceuses du Chat* would be an apt choice of piece to play. (How often, I wonder, and where in this country today *would* this be considered apt!) Each player has a B flat instrument only (not an uncommon state of affairs these days). You look at the first of the Stravinsky songs and you see that it is written for voice and three different types of clarinet, not a *single* one of which is possessed by your players! What are they? And what do you do? The answer is given in the exercises at the end of this chapter—an exercise on which a fair amount of judgment must be employed. This is an example of being both practical *and* enterprising.

The young conductor-producer or local musical leader *can* be enterprising if he uses to the full the intelligence and training which can come from a sound technical understanding and a confident sense of taste and discrimination. He must balance the choice between considering using sufficiently numerous and adequately

65

E

competent players—without perhaps being able to pay them—with insufficient and inadequate players—who may not need paying. Some useful tips are given in *Opera for Amateurs* by Frederick Woodhouse,[1] pp. 63-68. At least one should try to gather together the right instruments to interpret the composer's intentions, but even the correct instruments are worse than substitutes if they play above or below the note or before or after the beat.

These little songs of Stravinsky are a difficult enough adventure in combining enterprise with the hard facts of local conditions, but some works almost defy adaptation, even where the piano is brought in to fill-in. Such composers as Richard Strauss, Schoenberg and others writing at their peak about fifty years ago present a special difficulty because of a habit, now happily past, of writing gargantuan banquets of sound almost as a point of honour. Granville Bantock, for example in *Omar Khayyam* (1906), writes for double chorus, consisting of at least 200 voices, and a large orchestra which contains two complete string orchestras, each consisting of at least thirty players. The rest of the orchestration is on the lavish scale of the period: triple wood-wind, six horns, three trumpets, three trombones and tuba, timpani, three percussion players (to deal with bass drum, side drum, hand drum, cymbals, glockenspiel, triangle, tambourine, gong and camel-bell), two harps, organ ad lib. and three vocal soloists. One does feel that there is a danger in writing for such forces. After a time, the continued use, for example, of double string orchestra in ten parts can become an exercise in ingenuity in itself, which may be a substitute for clear musical thinking. Bantock is certainly very clever in his antiphonal use of the two bodies of strings and also of the two choirs, which by their careful

[1] Student's Music Library, Dobson, 1952.

placing in the hall, the composer expects to be divided again, making three or four separate choirs. The hand drum, incidentally, is played in the oriental manner, a difference being made in striking it with either the right or left hand. And yet this inflated score can be boiled down, since a vocal score has been made of the work.

10. In making a vocal (piano) score, the following considerations must be observed:

(a) The original instrumental layout must be preserved as far as possible, retaining the essential strands and rejecting the less important.

(b) The parts must lie under the hands of a modest pianist for rehearsal purposes.

(c) Orchestral devices must be changed into pianistic devices, i.e. rapidly repeated notes on strings are best changed to a tremolo of alternating notes at the keyboard.

(d) The piano part should be both a study for the man who wants to hear the musical effect of the whole at home and also a guide for the singers in rehearsal (remember the lesson learnt in Exercise 9 at the end of Chapter III).

11. Shall we say you have now decided what music will suit the people who can be gathered together to make vocal or orchestral music in your own district? You have taken no notice of (a) the lady who says, 'Oh dear, we couldn't do that. Far too difficult for Littletown', and (b) the gentleman who says, 'I remember *such* a nice performance of Stainer's *Crucifixion*. It would be so suitable in the parish church,' etc. If you are a musician, you decide *yourself* what can and should be done; and you balance the claims of the great music of the past with the worthy productions of the present. More vital: you decide how 'difficult', technically, the music should be. (A difficulty of idiom can be overcome by familiarity brought about by

67

persuasion.) The music can always be just that little bit more difficult than the players or singers are so far used to, so long as there is well-founded *enthusiasm* from the man-in-charge. Then you allocate solo parts where necessary—your programme is already to a certain extent built on the capabilities of your best singers and instrumentalists. You must naturally retain a mental impression of the effect of your worst performers in the most difficult passages and here it is best to plan in advance such things as tuttis, solo voices, first desks only of strings, doubling on the piano and other practical devices. When the rehearsals take place, planning is still most necessary. Suppose you have a single tenor trombone-player coming for the first time. First you discover whether he can read the tenor and bass clefs—it is quite possible that he has played his trombone in a brass band as a transposing instrument in B flat and from the *treble* clef. It is more than likely that this player is needed in only one or two items. The rehearsal time can be planned accordingly so that he need not be there all the time. If you cannot suit individuals in every instance, you should at least see that players are not kept twiddling their toes for long with nothing to do; and try always to avoid making experienced players repeat over and over again certain passages for the benefit of the slow, the novice or the stupid. Players and singers do much better when they come back from a tea-interval too. Now go ahead with all those willing people, the double bass with a new string, the bassoon with a sympathetically written-out part, the clarinet with a borrowed instrument, the trumpeter with a new understanding of how worth-while 'straight' music can be and all with a determination to make music themselves rather than accept it passively as a drug poured daily from a machine by the fireplace.

12. *Score-reading practice.*

It is not now to be supposed that the reader should be able glibly to sight-read at the piano the most complicated modern score. That is never fully possible—there are, after all, practical as well as intellectual limitations. Score-reading of any composition in an unfamiliar idiom can certainly be made easier—easier to 'fake', or suggest roughly, at the piano, that is—if the number of clefs and transpositions as well as the number of lines is reduced to a minimum. With regard to the former two points, see Appendix I; with regard to the latter, it has long been customary to write two instrumental parts on a single line and some scores, particularly Italian ones, write three parts together. This is not always quite satisfactory, even with the use of double-headed notes and also the figures 1, 2 and 3 to distinguish each player. There is still the likelihood of a jumbled appearance. When in doubt, it is never worth while to economize in paper. With trumpets, for example, write 1 and 2 together and write 3 on a separate stave. If the music is involved, either in rhythm or chromaticism, it is always best to write each part on a separate line. For reading practice, still not too difficult, try Vaughan Williams' *Household Music* (O.U.P., 1943). In the Variations on 'Aberystwyth', observe particularly that the theme is not stated by any single melodic strand, yet it *sounds* continuous (para. 7 above). Also the overlaps with their careful nuance markings are of the utmost value for study (para. 6 above). This composer, who has written for almost every instrument from the saxophone[1] to the harmonica,[2] indicates a number of alternatives in *Household Music*, which give a considerable choice in blending, and increase the chances of performance by a random

[1] In *Job*, 1930.
[2] *Romance*, 1952.

E*

gathering in a musical household. There are now two types of score-reading: the slow and careful study of a score and the reasonably quick performance. The second of these represents the activity of an acute perception, which when cultivated is in no respect a substitute for the other, but is an accomplishment in its own right.

13.   *The compass of some more instruments.*

(i) The written notes are given first.

(ii) The arrow indicates that the note is not the absolute limit.

(iii) For abbreviations of pitch, see p. 27.

Percussion Instruments with Notes of Definite Pitch:

Celesta	written c to c''''	(sounding c' to c''''')
Glockenspiel[1]	„ b♭ to c'''	(sounding b''♭ to c''''')
Xylophone	„ b'♭ to c''''	(but there are varieties of manufacture)

Timpani   ↙ F to f ↗

The other percussion instruments (those producing sounds of indefinite pitch) are mostly given in the list in Chapter I. Others are the gong (tam-tam), triangle and castanets. Constant Lambert, in *The Rio Grande* (1929), required these and also a keyed glockenspiel, small cowbell (without clapper), tenor drum, Chinese tom-tom, Chinese block and Turkish crash (one large suspended cymbal).

The Harp has a compass, nearly as large as the pianoforte's, from CC♭ to g''''♯. It should be pointed out that the strings of a harp are set in flats. By pressing named pedals, A to G, all the appropriate strings are made natural; by pressing further they are made sharp. N.B.— If you press, for example, the C pedal, *all* the C's on the instrument are sharpened.

[1] The B.B.C. Symphony Orchestra uses a resonator-amplified American instrument with a written compass from f to c".

Stringed Instruments	Harmonics up to:
Violin g to e'''' ↗	a'''' ↗
Viola c to a''' ↗	d'''' ↗
Cello C to e'' ↗	a''' ↗
Double bass ↙ E to c'' ↗ (sounding ↙ EE to c' ↗)	

N.B.—Some bass players tune their E string down to D. Others, very few, possess a lower string, which may be tuned to BB (sounding BBB). Natural (only) harmonics are possible up to f'' (this is the actual sound, which should be written and not transposed).

Harmonics for strings are written either (a) at the exact pitch with an 'o' above or (b) in a 'practical' way, the place where a finger stops the string with a round note and the place where another finger touches the string with a diamond (called artificial harmonics). Harmonics on the harp are given with a 'o' but the note written is an octave below the sound.

Most orchestration books vary considerably with regard to the prescribed upper limits of stringed instruments. The best test is the practical one: get a cellist friend to play the top e'' given here and then to go on upwards. You will see that there is still a good deal of finger-board left to play on, but the important snag is that the intervals get closer and closer together and the difficulty of playing in tune, especially in a jumpy passage becomes acute. This problem applies, of course, to the other stringed instruments and is accentuated in the equivalent part of the violin's compass, because the intervals are even smaller (less than the width of a finger).

QUESTIONS AND EXERCISES

1. (a) Write various chords and arpeggios for all stringed instruments demonstrating ease of performance in different positions.

(b) Write for strings and harp a 'spread' version of Chopin's Prelude in C minor, Op. 28, No. 20. (Do not forget that the pedals of the harp have to be reset for chromatic alteration.)

2. Obtain a score of Debussy's *La Mer* (1903-5), consider the first movement and

(a) Write an impression of the imagined effect of cellos and horns two bars before figure **9**, and again four and five bars after it.

(b) Study and describe the *pointilliste* scoring of page 17 and then write on two staves the basic melody and harmony (references are to the Durand miniature score).

3. Write in decorative style for string quartet based on the following scheme.

EXAMPLE 25a

Start as follows (write in *open* score):

EXAMPLE 25b

4. Orchestrate Grieg's *Norwegian Peasant Dance,* Op. 54, No. 2. Work approximately half of the piece and make judicious use of repeat marks. (N.B.—use of percussion—see para. 8).

5. Arrange the first song from Stravinsky's *Berceuses du Chat* for contralto with three B flat clarinets. N.B.—In addition to unravelling the various transpositions of the E flat clarinet, A clarinet and bass clarinet, you will have to transpose the whole piece up an appropriate amount (not necessarily the minimum). (Para. 9).

6. Taking Schubert, Piano Sonata No. 9 in A major. Op. posth. :

(a) Orchestrate the final twenty-seven bars of the first movement. To get the contrast effect of staccato left hand against legato right hand, study, for example, Beethoven's Symphony No. 7 in A—the last twenty-eight bars of the second movement—and make the left hand a complete string section and the right hand into wood-wind writing with horns. Do not be reticent about doubling at the octave in either, so long as the main melodic outlines are not obscured. In the arpeggio figures, sustained chords will be necessary to suggest the pedal and, in any case, to give 'depth'.

(b) Study the rate of chord change in the scherzo of this sonata and then orchestrate it.

7. (a) Produce a vocal score piano part from the figured bass of the opening four bars of Bach's Mass in B minor. (The miniature full score will be used for this. A standard vocal score can be used later for comparison.)

(b) Turn on to the instrumental passage six bars before the bass entry of the counter-exposition of the fugue (bar 75) and reduce these six bars to a piano part. (Again compare. This is six bars before the D in the vocal score. Are the overlaps adequately expressed?)

8. If you can get hold of a full score of Tchaikovsky's *Swan Lake* music, it might be worth turning to Odette's *pas seul* in Act II and noting the expressive imitations. Better still, look first at Granville Bantock's piano version (Paxton) and

73

try to reconstruct these imitations (which are there only *very* vaguely suggested) while orchestrating it yourself.

9. Look at the last bars of Sibelius's Fourth Symphony and compare the trumpets and trombones of the third to the ninth bars after letter **S** with the strings of the eleventh and twelfth bars after letter **T**. Is the string passage meant to sound like an echo of the brass passage? Write your views before listening to a recording or performance. Note especially the balance.

10. Orchestrate various movements from Mussorgsky's *Pictures at an Exhibition* and then compare with Ravel's version.

APPENDIX I

Copy of letter to The Musical Times, 2nd October, 1949.

Transposing Instruments.

I would like to go even further than Mr McNaught and see a change in the attitude to the printing of full scores and miniature scores both of old works and, particularly, of new compositions—doing away with transpositions in the scores while retaining them in the parts; and also in cases reducing the number of clefs. There are, as we are well aware, many pros and cons to be considered:

(1) Should we alter what the composer actually wrote? Well, we none of us read medieval music as it was written, nor do we read even Bach in all the clefs which he used and we are not prepared to share in Bach's problem with a transposing bassoon or Mozart's with a basset-horn. The way in which Berlioz and Wagner tackled the brass instruments' limitations is of great interest to the scholar, but I fail to see why we should all be irritated by their involved solutions every time we pick up a score while enjoying their music. With regard to clefs, the attitude of Orlando di Lasso was to choose a clef to suit the range of the voice or instrument, so that the notes would lie entirely on the five lines (in his two-part motets Lasso contrives imitation between the voices to *look* more or less in the same position on each stave). The tendency today, whether you like it or not, is to use treble and bass clefs only and supplement with ledger lines and the use of the 8va sign.

(2) How does the student get his training? By studying *old* editions, of course, just as he can study a medieval manuscript if he likes.

(3) Now the more practical side. What does the conductor

75

do about it? At present, he is supposed to be reading all the transposing instruments while the music is being played *correctly*. When the clarinet plays a wrong note, he tells him straight away what he should play, as the note in the score corresponds with that in the part. Now, in the new score advocated, the conductor does not have to transpose mentally all those parts all the time the music is correct; it is only when a *wrong* note is played that he has to make a quick mental transposition to tell the player his mistake—and no self-respecting conductor dare tell me that he can't do that.

(4) Then there is the copyist. The answer is that he should be paid more to transpose the necessary parts. The sooner the clarinets learn to play in C like everyone else, including, it may be mentioned, the modern trumpet player and many a willing hornist (whose Haydn Symphony parts are now being printed in F, but might as well be in C),[1] the better—and cheaper. Then the copyist will be charging extra only for the cor anglais, which remains a problem because oboists are not yet prepared to learn two sets of fingering. The old gag that you can tell where you are when you see the clarinet line in a different key no longer holds any water, since less and less music today is being written with key-signatures.

(5) There is no need for us to require a precedent, though, in fact, scores in the U.S.S.R. and America are now being printed with transposition eliminated; and the edition of Umberto Giordano (published by Ricordi), with treble and bass clefs only and no transposition, dates back to 1908. Also music of the Schoenberg school is usually printed without transposition—and no wonder.

(6) The old system has its advantages. I take classes in score-reading and shall continue to chuckle with devilish glee as I put the students through the most fiendish tests (but think it is high time we were all allowed to enjoy ourselves out of school). And, as a viola player, I would personally not like to lose the alto clef. However, the various matters should be

[1] I might add [1956] that as soon as F had become standardized for horns, the latest model, ironically, goes back to using B flat.

thrashed out at a conference. The case for the attack is not, as can be seen, a simple one, but I do feel that a start can be made with willingness and absence of prejudice.

(Signed) IAN PARROTT.

[*Note*—After the above letter was written, the new Penguin scores started eliminating transpositions.]

APPENDIX II

HINTS FOR THOSE WRITING IN SCORE

Use good ink with fairly thick pen for the music and a thinner pen for writing in the words. Have an ink eraser handy and also a sharp penknife.

First space out the bars in pencil. Make separations between groups of instruments. When there are two or more scores to a page try to get the bars of the lower *not* to look continuous with the upper; it is then easier for the reader to see that it is not *one* score on that page.

Use double treble clef or treble with an 8 under it for tenor voice (only when the chorus tenors are combined on one stave with the basses use the bass clef), but use the correct clefs for all instruments.

For triplets use a square bracket ⌐ 3 ⌐ to avoid confusion with phrasing.

Nuances (*f, p, cresc,* etc.) are written above voice parts, below instrumental parts and generally in the middle of a piano or other keyboard part (exceptionally, *pizz* and *arco* are written *above* string parts).

Reference figures or letters should be large and clear (before speed direction, if there is one). Underline speed directions. Write these above the top group and also above the strings.

Put words as near as possible under the notes and plan the spacing, i.e. with long words, start to the *left* of the notes.

Use ⎡ for chorus
⎨ for piano, for small groups and for divided instrumental lines (i.e. bracketing first and second trumpet or when the first violins are written on two lines).

Abbreviations for instruments should be as given in the table in Chapter I.

78

APPENDIX II

Unfortunately, the names of instruments and the abbreviations commonly used are not by any means standardized. For example, a glance at a few recent British scores reveals the following discrepancy in the lowest line alone: Double-bass, Double Bass, Double-basses, D.Bass, Contrabass, Contrabasses, Contrabbasses, Contrabasso, Contra-Basso, Contrabassi, Bass, Basses, Bassi, String Bass, C.B., Cb.

SOME RECOMMENDED BOOKS

Cecil Forsyth: *Orchestration*, Macmillan, 1914; 30/-
Harold C. Hind: *The Orchestra and Its Instruments*, Boosey & Hawkes, 1936; 5/6
William Lovelock: *Orchestral Score-Reading*, Hammond, 1952
Percy M. Young: *Handbook of Choral Technique*, Dobson, 1953; 6/-
Gordon Jacob: *How to Read a Score*, Boosey & Hawkes, 1944; 3/-
H. A. Chambers: *Musical Manuscript*, Curwen, 1951; 5/-
J. Raymond Tobin: *Self-Help in Aural Tests*, J. Williams, 1948
Walter Piston: *Orchestration*, Gollancz, 1955; 21/-.

INDEX OF INSTRUMENTS AND PERSONS

82

INDEX OF WORKS FOR STUDY

Titles of Books are italicized

84